~ Sunny Side Up ~
~ Eggshells to Seashells ~

By Olivia Valency

ISBN: 979-8-9946200-9-0

This publication is designed to provide accurate and authoritative information regarding the subject matter covered. It is sold with the understanding that neither the author nor the publisher is engaged in rendering legal, investment, accounting, mental health, religious, or other professional services. While the publisher and author have used their best efforts in preparing this book, they make no representations or warranties concerning the accuracy or completeness of the contents of this book and specifically disclaim any implied warranties of merchantability or fitness for a particular purpose. No warranty may be created or extended by sales representatives or written sales materials. The advice, opinions, beliefs, and strategies contained herein may not be suitable for your situation. You should consult with a professional when appropriate. Neither the publisher nor the author shall be liable for any loss of profit or any other commercial damages, including but not limited to special, incidental, consequential, personal, or other damages.

Any mention of Calvinism is specific to the church where I grew up and how I recall it being taught to me by my mother, teachers, and preachers throughout my life. It's not always taught the same way in all Calvinist churches.

For privacy reasons, some names, locations, and dates may have been changed.

First edition, March 2026

Books written by Olivia Valency

Scrambled Eggs ~ Walking on Shells

Sunny Side Up ~ Eggshells to Seashells

Deviled Eggs ~ Shells in the Yolk

Poached Eggs ~ Selling Empty Shells

Over Easy ~ Cracking the Shell

Special thanks to my daughters,
Hannah and Heather,
for proofreading and editing.

TABLE OF CONTENTS

~ Sink or Swim ~

Sunny Side Up is a choice. We can either *sink or swim.* For many years, I had been sinking. Whenever I tried to come up for air, someone was always pushing my head back down. Throughout my life, I've endured and suffered many traumas and abuses. I grew up in an abusive home and was married to an abuser for 23 years. I have 41 years of experience dealing with various types of abuse, loss, trauma, and destructive behavior. My focus here is on how I became Sunny Side Up, so I only share a glimpse of what I endured. The detailed traumas of my childhood and marriage are in my other book, "Scrambled Eggs, Walking on Shells."

Over the years, I often struggled with situational depression. Many times, I was at zero on my happiness scale. The waterfall of tears I cried could fill several bathtubs. As time went on, I stopped using tissues to blow my nose and wipe my tears. Instead, I went straight for the kitchen towel. Breaking free into the sunshine felt impossible. It was a long and difficult journey. After years of suffering, I finally came out on the other side of the waterfall.

It's surprising how pain can shape your personality. You might notice in my writing that I'm a straightforward, no-nonsense, facts-only type of person. That trait comes from being lied to so often that I can no longer tolerate wishy-washy, vague, or beat-around-the-bush communication. Countless lies caused my mind to spin. I was never sure what was true or false. Over time, I became intolerant of lies. We all deserve honesty, so I strive to give honest and direct communication. I prefer this, so I give that to others.

I know what pain feels like, and I understand how difficult it is to leave abusers. Seeing the strength and determination I have now might offer you hope. It may encourage you to escape your harmful situation. If you can't escape today, keep your eye on the end of the rainbow. One of these days, I'll meet you on the other side of the waterfall.

Now, I feel grateful for all my experiences. They have shaped me into who I am today. I'm thankful for the wisdom I've gained. It allows me to help others. All those hurts and pains gave me a clear understanding of what the opposite of love looks like. They also showed me what true love really is. These experiences have taught me to appreciate love on a much deeper level. I now realize that love is the most important virtue to achieve, so that we never hurt ourselves or others.

Many outside anchors suppressed and trampled on my joy. I found that as I started removing those life-sapping vultures, my happiness increased. Once I recognized this, there was no stopping me! My go-getter personality wouldn't let me rest until I reached the top. I removed all negative things and harmful people who were dragging me down. I had to choose whether to *sink or swim,* and I decided to *swim.*

To remove the negative influences from my life, I focused on being assertive. I first learned about assertiveness and its importance when I was in the hospital for an eating disorder as a teenager. Since then, I have practiced whenever a situation arose. I researched online and watched videos on many self-help topics, including assertiveness. However, I won't have it perfected by the time I die. Sometimes, I still mess up and react with anger instead of assertiveness. However, even in my stumbling, I'm doing my best. That's 100 times better than doing nothing at all.

Assertiveness became my shield of protection. I became skilled at recognizing harmful things and people. I had to build confidence to stand up for myself and be honest about what I needed. There could be no beating around the bush. It took courage to say what was best for me. I had to become brave and express my true feelings. Masks would not cut the mustard. Everyone was going to see the genuine me.

I learned to trust my instincts and focused on what my gut told me. When it said someone was unkind, I responded immediately by calling them out on their words. Trust me, this wasn't easy. Fear of confrontation often rose in my chest, and I worried that an argument might start or that I was being argumentative. I questioned whether I was wrong or if I had misunderstood. Over time, I learned that my gut is 100% correct.

It's best to clarify questionable words right away so the abuser can't later misconstrue their words. Waiting until tomorrow or next week to confront them gives them time to make up excuses. Often, they'll make you doubt your memory or claim they didn't mean it that way.

Most abusers never accept personal responsibility. If they did, they would have to change. They like who they are, and their bad behavior has served them well for years. I call them out by asking, "What did you say?" or "What did you mean by that?" Often, to save face, they reply, "Oh, nothing." Not letting them get away with their hurtful comments, I then say, "I feel hurt you said that to me."

Calling out harm and requesting an apology is the best way to prevent internal turmoil from festering inside us for days or weeks. It takes practice to say, "I feel hurt." Addressing hurtful behavior is standing up for ourselves. We need to practice self-love and to stand up for ourselves. Practice makes perfect.

This person isn't necessary in my life. I can handle life on my own. The only people I allow in are those who aren't negative, vulgar, or harmful to me.

I worked on being assertive while married to Dale. At first, I let him respond with excuses, accusations, and arguments. This often turned into a three-hour-long fight. Today's issue was swept under the rug. He blindsided me with allegations from years ago. He would say anything to avoid taking responsibility for his actions.

I became frustrated because he always changed the subject. He turned it back on me and made it my fault. I learned how to handle this behavior. If he brought up past topics, I raised my hand to stop him. I said, "I only want to discuss this one issue and nothing else!" I then repeated my initial grievance. After a few tries, I got him to stop. Many times, he stormed out of the room. He was unwilling to address his hurtful actions.

Dale's storming off was also hurtful. He refused to apologize. I asked if there was a good time to talk about what was bothering me. He said, "No time is a good time." His obvious, uncaring attitude hurt my feelings. I ignored him until he would discuss the pain in my heart.

A day or two later, he tried talking to me as if nothing had happened. I wouldn't let him off the hook. I told him that nothing can return to normal until we address the issue. Nothing got swept under the rug. Dale's childhood abuse followed him into adulthood. He brought the same destructive behavior into our marriage. It was a way of life. It was all he knew. I felt sorry for his experience and thought I could fix him, but I didn't realize that everyone has to fix themselves.

Despite my efforts, nothing I ever said changed Dale. He pretended to be different, but within a week, he returned to the same ol' dirty Dale. I tried to make my marriage work for 23 years. Near the end, I told Dale that I could no longer tolerate his behavior. Dale chose a different path, with another wife. He was a broken toaster. All he gave me was a bunch of burnt toast!

Being assertive is expressing ourselves in a calm, honest, kind, and direct way. It's not condescending, loud, or aggressive. It's standing up for ourselves and calling out harmful actions. Assertiveness is saying, "I feel hurt" and "No, thank you." It's letting others know they may not hurt us. We protect that "10" on our happiness scale.

Aggressive, passive-aggressive, and abusive people often dislike assertiveness. They dislike boundaries and don't want us to stand up for ourselves. If someone doesn't respect my boundaries, they can't be in my *swimming pool.* Allowing them in always decreases my happiness.

When making decisions, if I'm in doubt, I don't do it. I can always change my mind later. For some decisions, if I feel uncertain, I use a coin-flip trick to see what my instincts say. Heads means yes, tails means no. I pay attention to how my gut reacts to the coin's answer. If I don't like the result, then I have my answer. If my gut likes the answer, then that's what is right for me. My gut knows deep down what's best for me.

When practicing assertiveness, I include "please," "thank you," and "I" statements. Using "you" statements can seem accusatory and can lead to arguments. Some examples of "I feel" statements are:

I feel hurt. *I feel pain in my heart. *I feel scared. *I feel belittled. *I feel offended. *I feel discounted. *I feel berated. *I feel lonely. *I feel happy. *I feel judged. *I feel criticized. *I feel overwhelmed. *I feel content. *I feel sad. *I feel scatterbrained. *I feel rushed.

It's hard to argue with "I feel" statements. If someone tries to argue, I say, "There's nothing to discuss here. I'm only expressing how I feel," or "Feelings aren't right or wrong. It's just how I feel right now." You could also say, "I'm not looking for an argument. I'm just exercising my God-given right to share my feelings." If they keep trying to debate, you can tell them, "I'm not available for this conversation."

It's difficult to escape from abusive people, especially once married and with children. It's best to recognize hurtful people early to avoid them. Not all aggressive or passive-aggressive actions make someone irredeemable. If they apologize, they may stay in my life. However, if they don't offer a sincere apology, they have to go.

If someone is causing you physical harm, I recommend contacting the police. It's tough to do, but love shouldn't be painful. If they are hitting you, they are not loving you. They are trying to control you through violence. Loving ourselves means not letting anyone hurt us.

When I was married to Dirty Dale, he hit me once early in our marriage. I went to the neighbor to call the pastor of our church. Dale never hit me again. He knew I'd tell. I don't permit anyone to abuse me anymore. However, it took time to reach that point. I filled several bathtubs with my tears and used many kitchen towels.

Abusers are emotional vampires who drain you dry. Don't cast your light into the black holes disguised as people. Stop playing their game and detach from their drama. I've learned that it's best not to react, but only respond with calm, assertive truth, facts, and "I feel" statements. I don't fall for fake apologies either. We can turn our pain into the power of loving ourselves enough to stop engaging. It's better to walk away and remove them from our lives.

After enduring extreme cruelty, I have no patience or tolerance for abusive people. Loving myself has made me so resilient that no one can break me again. I've become whole within myself and no longer rely on validation from others to feel complete. I am now careful about where I direct my love, which is a healthy way to protect myself from harm. All my past suffering and wounds have become the raw material that has shaped my wisdom today.

I never needed or wanted revenge. Becoming a powerhouse of love for myself was reward enough. I moved into a mansion on the hill. Meanwhile, all the abusers still live in muddy straw shacks down by the swamp. I hope they find deep love for themselves someday. Without it, they will drown, as I almost did. Thank goodness I chose to *swim!*

Although it was my path, you don't have to endure such pain to become a powerhouse of love for yourself. You can live in the mansion on the hill. Choose to *swim.* Love yourself deeply and completely. Learn how to become your own best friend.

~ The Wind Beneath My Wings ~

After my divorce, I began dating. After several attempts to find companionship, I realized my life is more peaceful without a partner. I couldn't find anyone who was spiritually and mentally in sync with me. It was time for me to stay single — at least for now.

I realized that being my own best friend is the *wind beneath my wings.* I've even given myself a couple of sweet nicknames. Whenever I need comfort or praise, I talk to myself using these nicknames. I take care of myself emotionally. I've become my own best friend to the point where I don't depend on outside friends or validation.

At our core, we are all basically the same. Everyone experiences similar emotions, wants, needs, and desires, though to different degrees. We all require food, water, shelter, and sleep. Everyone experiences happiness, contentment, excitement, gratitude, and hope. Likewise, we all feel sadness, anxiety, anger, and fear. Each of us has similar emotional needs for love, praise, comfort, positive reinforcement, encouragement, and forgiveness.

It's important to care for ourselves. Our physical needs — such as cleaning ourselves, eating well, and wearing comfortable clothing — are essential. However, the most important thing is to attend to our emotional needs. We must show kindness, patience, and forgiveness toward ourselves.

Using my nickname and talking to myself keeps me connected to my inner child. It's my responsibility to make sure she is a 10 on her happiness scale. If she's not, it's my fault. That means I'm not taking care of her as she needs. She needs lots of love, and it's my job to give it to her. My inner child is my favorite person in the whole wide world.

My name is Olivia, and my nicknames are Liv and Livvy. I have become Livvy's best friend and take care of her. She is my top priority, and I feel a deep sense of loyalty to her. Being her protector, I am always there for her whenever she needs me. I show her kindness and love through positive, gentle words. I treat her with patience, understanding, and forgiveness. Livvy deserves the best love in the world and is to be treated with honor and respect. I love her deeply and completely.

I allow Livvy to feel all of her emotions. If she feels sad, I ask, "Liv, what is going on? Why are you feeling sad?" The reason always comes to mind, and I comfort Livvy, helping her through her sadness. I tell her, "Yes, I understand. I'm sorry you are feeling this way. What can we do to make this better?" I suggest some options and pick the one I think will work best.

Sometimes, all I need is a gentle tapping on my energy points to release the bzzzt in my energy system. I'll explain this in more detail later. In short, it involves light tapping while acknowledging my feelings of sadness, anxiety, or fear. During this, I affirm that I deeply and completely love myself. This Emotional Freedom Technique has been a lifesaver for me.

I listen to what my body and heart need. If Livvy needs to cry, I cry with her. Putting my hand on my heart and chest, I hold her until she feels better. I'll do whatever it takes to help Livvy through her sadness. I tell her, "I love you, Livvy." Whenever I accomplish a task, I tell her, "Great job, Livvy! You did great! I'm very proud of you!" I'm her best friend, and I won't let anyone hurt her ever again. She has endured more than her share of pain. She won't be getting any more of that! I, Olivia, will make sure of that!

I treat Livvy respectfully. Just as I want others to treat me with respect, I'm quick to give Livvy the utmost respect. I'm never demanding of her. I always say please and thank you. She's never been mean to me, so why would I ever be mean to her? She has such a beautiful heart. All she desires is to be loved, comforted, respected, forgiven, and appreciated. I'm the *wind beneath her wings.*

If I ever mistreat her, I always offer her a sincere apology. I tell her, "I'm so sorry, Livvy. You didn't deserve that. You deserve the best. I'll try hard not to do that again." She forgives me right away because my apology is genuine, and because I'm her best friend. We are two peas in a pod. Plus, I was the one who helped her escape from the prison of hell she was in. She's forever grateful to me for that.

I can't be hard on myself. Every day, I do my best. If I learn to do something better tomorrow, I'll start doing it better then. Yesterday, I didn't know better, so I can't be mad at myself. I didn't come out of my mother's womb with an instruction manual. We're all flying by the seat of our pants here. Life is more of a learning adventure. We learn as we go.

I express gratitude for what I've learned from my mistakes. Mourning and lamenting over the actions I took yesterday, when I didn't know better, suggests I was supposed to be perfect. That sets expectations too high, as no one can live a life without mistakes. Everyone makes mistakes. We're all doing our best as we stumble through life. We should never judge others for their mistakes, as their mistakes are just different from ours.

I've learned that it's best to forgive ourselves for past mistakes and perceived failures. We can't remain stuck in the coulda, woulda, and shoulda mindset. I was the best daughter and wife that I knew how to be. As a mother, I raised my children to the best of my ability. I did my best with everything I had. Whoever my children choose to be from this point on is their own decision. I love them all, and I'll support them in whatever they need. I have a respectful and kind relationship with all of them. However, they are their own person now. Who they are and what mistakes they make is none of my business. Fly, little birdie, fly. You do you, and I'll do me.

I practice positive self-talk with my inner child, investing in myself. Change only happens when we embrace our true selves. I take full responsibility for my emotional well-being. No one else can care for me the way I need to be cared for. Others don't know the words we need to hear. They don't know the exact love and comfort we seek. But we do, and it's our responsibility to provide that for ourselves.

Only we know what praise and level of kindness we require. Everyone has a lot going on in their lives. They are busy attending to their own needs and trying to meet their emotional requirements. They don't know what we need for comfort or praise. It's best to learn how to do that for ourselves and stop relying on others. I don't wait for others to praise me. It's my job to blow my own whistle.

Peace, joy, love, and happiness are within ourselves. The primary key to being Sunny Side Up is to treat ourselves with love, patience, and forgiveness — and be our own best friend.

I give myself positive reinforcement, encouragement, love, comfort, praise, and forgiveness. Many people believe they should not love themselves. Someone taught them that self-love is egotistical and vain. I had to reprogram and retrain my brain.

Repetition is key to retraining your brain. At first, it might feel as if you're lying to yourself. You may feel like a fish out of water, but don't let that stop you. Others have told you not to love yourself or that you're unworthy of love. You will need to lie to yourself repeatedly until loving yourself becomes second nature. That's what they did to us, so we must do the opposite to undo their lies.

One effective method during this retraining phase is to write positive affirmations on a sticky note. Stick them on your refrigerator or bathroom mirror. Write things like, *I am beautiful. *Me and Livvy, two peas in a pod. *I love you, Livvy. *Me and Liv, best friends forever. Whenever we pass by our notes, we read them and feel the joy they bring. It helps retrain our brains to accept the truth. It may feel strange or embarrassing at first. You might resist it. But stay persistent until it feels natural. Repetition is key — repetition, repetition, repetition.

Once you overcome the lies and embrace this beautiful love for yourself, you will never look back. It feels wonderful and right. Be the *wind beneath your wings.* Jump onto the rainbow. There's a pot of gold waiting on the other side. The best relationship you'll ever have is the one you build with yourself. Become vulnerable, sharing every thought and feeling with yourself. You won't sweep anything under the rug again because now you have a best friend to help you handle it all.

Tell yourself things like, *Livvy, I'm your best friend. *Livvy, I promise I won't let anyone hurt you ever again. *Liv, you deserve the best, and I'll give you all the love and kindness you need. *Livvy, I'm here for you always. I've got your back, and I'll always stand up for you. *Liv, you have such a beautiful heart. I love you! *Livvy, it's you and me, best friends forever — two peas in a pod.

Olivia is the powerhouse. She goes to the ends of the earth to protect and love little Livvy. If you hurt Livvy, Olivia will call you out on it. If you don't give her a sincere apology, Olivia will remove you from her life. No one will ever hurt sweet little Livvy again!

~ Sail Your Own Ship ~

Loving ourselves means being proud of our accomplishments. Pride is essential for our self-worth. I take pride in everything I do and feel proud of my achievements. After completing a task, I take the time to praise myself.

I also thank our Heavenly Father for His help. Validation from myself and my Heavenly Father is all I need. We would be nothing and have nothing if not for our Heavenly Father. He created us and this beautiful earth for us to enjoy. He loves all of His children. Poppa created us to give Him pleasure. It pleases Him when we love Him, ourselves, and others. He loves nice brown buttery toast — with a little bit of honey or a little bit of jam.

We need to decide who deserves to be our friend. A true friend treats us with the same kindness and love that we show ourselves. To find compatible companions, we first have to know ourselves. I made a list describing my qualities and standards. It helped me evaluate who is a good fit for me. It looks something like this:

*I am dependable, honest, moral, and decent. *I show love, patience, and kindness. *I keep my word and honor my commitments. *I'm not an introvert. *I'm not sarcastic. *I say please and thank you. *I speak from my heart. *I'm assertive. *I acknowledge my feelings and share them. *I have a positive attitude. *I don't complain. *I'm a problem solver who looks for positive solutions. *I'm a go-getter, a hustler. *I have a clean sense of humor. *I don't do drugs or gamble. *I'm a good listener and an excellent communicator. *I'm straightforward. *I take responsibility for my actions. *I'm a leader, self-motivated, and I take the initiative. *I get things done and don't waste time. *I'm a problem solver and know how to fix things. *I'm proactive, dedicated, and trustworthy. *I'm reliable and responsible. *I'm genuine, generous, and I set boundaries. *I use self-praise. *I don't make my bed in the mornings. *I'm mostly organized.

The more you describe yourself, the better your chances are of recognizing these qualities in others — or the lack thereof. I suggest writing fifty traits, but one hundred isn't too many. It saves a lot of heartache to have our standards set beforehand. That way, we won't allow any dirty birds into our lives.

We should take off our muddy boots when entering someone else's home or a public space. Vulgarity, sarcasm, arguing, and attacking others should stay at the door. Everyone deserves respect. Anyone who treats me with disrespect can't be in my life. Keeping the mud out of our house, life, and mind brings peace.

Using derogatory slurs is harmful. Everyone is beautiful and unique. Acting superior because of religious beliefs, gender, ethnicity, skin color, accent, heritage, or location is hurtful. We are all children of our Heavenly Father. He created us perfectly, and He loves us all equally.

Everyone is on a path of learning. We shouldn't judge, condemn, or criticize others. Instead, we can teach others to love themselves and be their own best friend. We hurt people if we are mean, impatient, sarcastic, or talk negatively about them behind their backs.

I ask myself, if Jesus were standing right beside me, how would I treat others? That's how we should treat ourselves and others. A rule I follow is to do good, not hurt others, mind my own business, and enjoy my journey.

It's important to keep our word and be dependable. We don't want to be known as liars. Our actions show who we are based on whether we keep our word. Our word should be as valuable as gold. Everyone should trust it as if they were taking it to the bank. If our word isn't good, then we aren't trustworthy or reliable. Once we give our word, it's essential to keep it, except in emergencies. That way, others can trust us. It's also how we earn respect for ourselves. When we give our word, it's like shaking hands on it — a spoken contract.

Loving ourselves is the solution our world needs. We can each become the change within ourselves. We should focus on ourselves and care for our emotional, spiritual, physical, and financial well-being. *Sail your own ship.* Cheer yourself on. Praise yourself. Everything you need is inside you.

When we reach the pot of gold at the end of our rainbow, we enter a state of bliss. When our cup of love is full, it overflows onto others. Practice patience and compassion for those who continue to suffer. However, don't try to fix them, and don't let them into your bubble of peace, joy, love, and happiness. We may feel sorry for them, as they may have been in this mental state for years. In passing, we can plant a small seed to show them how to love themselves. That's the only way we can help them. It's not wise to get involved with them. If they don't love themselves, they will always lower our level of happiness.

Loving ourselves involves being responsible. We can *sail our own ship* by working hard, setting clear goals, and managing our finances carefully. Completing a task gives us an incredible sense of pride. With each success, we should praise ourselves for a job well done. Using my nickname, I say, "Livvy, great job! I'm very proud of you!"

Giving up isn't an option. If I fail, I try again. Albert Einstein failed thousands of times before he got the light bulb to work. If I don't know how, I do more research. I might set it aside for a while, but I always come back to it. We can accomplish anything we set our minds to.

I enjoy being frugal. I avoid buying unnecessary items because they just create clutter. Kids don't need 25 gifts for Christmas or their birthday. I am diligent in paying off my debts. I eat healthy and sometimes prepare a large casserole to store leftovers in freezer bags for future meals.

I use the phrases "please" and "thank you." I show appreciation for everything others do for me. When someone says, "Thank you," I reply, "You're welcome." If someone asks me if I want something, I say, "Yes, please," or "No, thank you."

When I ask for something, I use a polite tone because I am requesting a favor. It's my responsibility to take care of my needs. When someone demands things from me, it feels rude. I never ask others for things I can do on my own. It's not anyone else's job to do things for me. I have the ability and working legs, so I take care of myself. It's not my right to boss anyone around or to have them at my beck and call. I *sail my own ship!*

~ Hidden Treasure ~

Forgiving ourselves becomes easier when we realize that everyone else makes mistakes. Forgiving ourselves is a vital part of loving ourselves. We show love to ourselves by being gentle, patient, and forgiving of our own errors. Love and forgiveness toward ourselves are the miracles that transform our lives and help our garden grow beautifully.

Much mental turmoil and physical illness result from not forgiving ourselves. We can release our mental burden by using self-forgiveness and by filling our hearts with love.

We all make many mistakes. Mistakes are necessary for learning and growth. They lead us to a deeper understanding and wisdom within ourselves. When we embrace and are thankful for our mistakes, it helps us get to know ourselves better. It's important to find the silver lining in every mistake, as each one contains a *hidden treasure.* When we discover the lesson, we become grateful for the experience. What wisdom have we gained? Now, how can we use our newfound understanding to help others? What did we learn to do better next time? Our mistakes can help us flourish, grow, and become a light to others.

When we make a mistake, it's important to take responsibility for our actions. To be forgiven, we need to ask for forgiveness. Be genuine, with no fake apologies. Express our sincere sorrow by saying, "I'm sorry." Tell them we'll try never to do it again. Also, saying "I love you" helps them heal. Skipping the word "I" and only saying "sorry" isn't taking full responsibility. The words "I'm sorry" carry a much more heartfelt meaning. It shows we are taking complete responsibility. The same applies to "I love you." Removing the word "I" takes away much of the personal meaning behind the words.

It's preferable to receive forgiveness when we ask for it. People might choose not to forgive, but it's still important to find the silver lining. Once we recognize what we've learned, we can feel thankful for the lesson. Then, we can move forward in forgiving ourselves. We are all on a journey of learning. We all hurt others, whether we mean to or not. Our Heavenly Father expected us to make mistakes. We didn't come with an instruction manual. I've found that discovering the lesson in my mistakes — *the hidden treasure* — and forgiving myself helps me keep putting one foot in front of the other.

I tell myself, *Livvy, I forgive you. *We'll do better next time. *I've learned so much from this mistake. *I'm thankful for the lesson and the deeper insight. *I can now help others.

It's easy to forgive others when they are sorry. I forgive people who come to me with a genuine apology. If they aren't sincere, they'll do it again. I protect my heart from them. I forgive them in my heart, but I don't pursue a relationship or try to fix them. Many people hurt others because they don't love themselves. They haven't learned love and kindness. We need to protect ourselves from them.

I avoid arguing because I see it as a waste of energy. I listen carefully and try to find a small piece of wisdom to hold on to. It doesn't make much sense to be mean or argue over someone's beliefs today because their opinions might change tomorrow. We might learn something valuable from them. We can feel thankful for having talked to that person and gained a little *hidden treasure.* I keep the flower, plant it in my garden, and discard the rest. A rule I live by is, "You do you, and I'll do me." I mind my own business. Life's an adventure, and I enjoy every moment I can.

When going through trauma, playing Tetris helps reduce suffering and aftereffects. Journaling is also helpful. Practicing gratitude is very healing. I've learned to turn negative thoughts into positive ones by expressing gratitude. The more grateful we are, the more positive we become. Gratitude is key to keeping a positive outlook. After any trauma or loss, such as divorce or the death of a loved one, finding fifty things each day to feel grateful for can help ease grief and pain in our hearts.

I'm thankful for my food, water, and home. *I'm thankful for the sunshine and the rain. *I'm thankful for my tears, both of happiness and pain. *I'm thankful for my eyes, ears, nose, fingers, and toes. *I'm thankful for the birds and the bees. *I'm thankful for the flowers, grass, and trees. *I'm thankful for my car and the pavement to walk and drive on. *I'm thankful for my shower, bath, and bed. *I'm thankful for my coffee and my tea. *I'm thankful for my toilet and that I can pee. *I'm thankful I can feel, hear, smell, and taste. *I'm thankful for wisdom, knowledge, and understanding. *I'm thankful for my friends and children. *I'm thankful for my job and the ability to work, walk, and run. *I'm thankful for my puzzle and the ability to read. *I'm thankful for our Heavenly Father, who created us perfectly and loves us all.

Be specific and speak with deep feeling when saying, "I am so thankful for…" The more gratitude we express, the less negative and sad we feel. Gratitude is positivity. It's the *hidden treasure* that weeds out the negativity. Gratitude and negativity cannot coexist in the same garden. One stays. The other goes.

~ Pearly Gates ~

Loving ourselves is protecting ourselves from physical, emotional, or verbal harm. Happiness doesn't come from having vulgar, negative, or hurtful people in our lives. Our goal is to reach that 10 on our happiness scale. That means we must eliminate all hurtful things and people. We can't allow anyone into our lives who will lower our happiness level. When we love ourselves, our relationship with ourselves and our Heavenly Father is all we need. Anyone else should treat us with the same love and respect we give ourselves. Otherwise, out they go.

We can't hold on to others tightly. We must let go of those who are harmful. If we don't release them, we will suffer. Practice holding people loosely. Loving ourselves and being our own best friend is enough. We don't need to add harmful people to our lives to increase our happiness. It's important to understand that everyone who enters our lives will inevitably hurt us, in one way or another, whether they mean to or not. We can expect this from everyone. Likewise, we will unintentionally hurt others. If we do hurt someone, it's important to apologize.

We all have a small garden of peace, joy, love, and happiness inside us. Many people forget to close their *Pearly Gates,* and they allow harmful weeds into their gardens. These weeds choke out our happiness. Although it can be difficult, we must grab our weed whackers and remove these weeds.

Then we can breathe freely again. It's my responsibility to protect little Livvy.

The only people I allow in my garden are those who treat me with love and respect. Only those who give sincere apologies may enter my *Pearly Gates.* I don't fear hurtful people. I have a perfectly good weed whacker to remove them from my garden. Whenever I meet a new person, I analyze them to see if they show love. Looking back now, why did I ever let unloving people into my little bubble of peace, joy, love, and happiness? Ahhh, I didn't know better.

Only those who take responsibility for their actions may enter my garden. Protecting my little bubble, I am selective about who and what I let in. Hurtful people decrease my happiness. If they insist on coming in, I explain why they can't enter. I stand my ground and protect my garden from thistles and thorns.

Vulgar, disrespectful, and hateful people are in a state of hell. If they attempt to bring their hell into my bubble of heaven, my *Pearly Gates* are closed. I always evaluate who can enter and who must leave.

The main reason we tolerate hurtful people in our lives is that we aren't loving ourselves. When we love and respect ourselves, we expect the same from others. In my experience, nine out of ten people aren't giving themselves the love they need. Nine out of ten will hurt themselves and us as well.

We can't force others to improve their behavior. Every person must change from within themselves. If they modify their actions just to please us, or out of fear of losing us, their change won't last. In a few days, they'll return to who they are. They are who they are, who they are, who they are.

They are exhibiting unacceptable behavior, so I must weed them out. It has nothing to do with the person — only behavior, behavior, behavior. Someday, they might learn to love themselves. We can decide then whether we want them back in our lives. Until they choose love, they need to stay on the sidelines. Hurtful people can't be anywhere near little Livvy.

I know that it's difficult to remove people. I portray the simple process of removal because I've learned how to do it quickly. It took me years to figure out how to do it immediately. I stayed in my marriage for 23 years before I was able to escape. I felt I had to stay for financial reasons and for the sake of the kids, as I didn't want to break up their family. I made plans and prepared for the day I could be free. It's often a long, painful journey, filled with grief and suffering. Even removing the harmful weeds causes a different wave of grief and sadness — especially when it involves family.

I've distanced myself from some of my sisters to protect my peace. We grew up in an abusive home, church, and community. They have carried that abuse forward. They haven't yet found the path of love. I still feel the pain of letting them go. However, the sadness I feel today is better than the grief caused by their harm. I look forward to the day when they realize love is the answer. When that happens, I'll be here with open arms.

If anyone lowers my level of happiness, I keep them at a distance. I love them from afar, hoping they'll choose love.

However, I don't let them dump their bird turds on me. They aren't on the path of love, and I can't make them want it. Until they change from within, they remain a threat to me and my well-being.

We can offer a caring and attentive ear to those facing occasional struggles. However, some people drain our time with negativity and complaints. I choose to distance myself from them because they drain my energy and happiness. It's important to guard our *Pearly Gates* — once someone is inside, it's hard to remove them.

We can suggest to them what we would do in their situation. We can teach them to love, respect, and forgive themselves. Additionally, we can guide them to eliminate harmful people from their lives or help them find the silver lining in their experience. If none of that works, we can tell them how their behavior affects us. That might help. However, if it doesn't, we can become too busy or choose not to answer the phone as often.

Don't worry if they can't hear your message of love, respect, and forgiveness. They may need to experience more pain before they can take action. They may need to hit rock bottom on their happiness scale before they can hear you. I had to hit rock bottom many times before I figured it out.

Standing up for ourselves isn't easy — especially with family. Remember, our true family and friends are those who treat us with love and respect. If they don't, we can't consider them family or friends. Blood doesn't matter when it comes to addressing harmful actions. I will protect Livvy, no matter what the cost.

Resist the urge to respond emotionally to people's outbursts. For some, all they know is to lash out with emotion. They are hurting and feeling sorry for themselves. They haven't learned how to love and comfort themselves. Never learning to focus on the facts, they let emotions cloud their judgment. We can comfort them with the truth. We can tell them we're sorry they are hurting.

It's important to feel all of our emotions. However, I've learned to separate emotions from facts. This helps me handle situations in a clear, kind, and assertive way. My decisions are based on truth, reason, and common sense. I look at the facts and the plausible reasons to give the benefit of the doubt. I try to find a solution: What happened? Who hurt me? Did they give a sincere apology when I told them I felt hurt? If yes, they can stay. If no, they must go. Easy cheesy. Now I can return to crying about it if I need to.

Emotions interfere with our ability to respond appropriately. It's important to have a healthy response prepared in case someone is hurtful.

If it's helpful to you, write the following on a piece of paper. Hang it on the fridge, or keep it in your wallet. Pull it out for reference when someone is cruel. Here's an example of what your paper would look like: 1) Recognize that the person was cruel. 2) Remember that cruel people don't love themselves. 3) To avoid overreacting, ask for clarification. Say, "What did you say?" or "What did you mean by that?" or "Why did you do or say that to me?" 4) Say, "I feel hurt that you did or said that to me." 5) If they don't apologize, say, "I deserve an apology for that." 6) If they apologize, forgive them. 7) If they refuse to apologize, tell them, "I don't allow hurtful people in my life. I have to put you on the sidelines. You may come to me if you decide to apologize."

It's important to address hurtful actions promptly. In a kind, assertive tone, let people know when they've caused harm. They might apologize, blame you, or snub you and walk away. It's best not to engage in arguments. Keep the conversation focused on this one hurt. I don't ignore issues or sweep things under the rug. Sometimes, the person who snubbed me returns to talk to me. They pretend nothing happened. I tell them the pain is still there. I let them know that the hurt needs to be resolved before I allow any further conversation. The *Pearly Gates* are closed — I don't let them back into my life until they give me a genuine apology.

Psychopaths, narcissists, and passive-aggressive people will try to shift the blame onto you. They make it your fault that they hurt you. They'll never admit to hurting you or give a sincere apology. The best they might offer is a fake apology. Doubtful, but maybe. Don't chase after an apology. Run as fast as you can before they suck you into their vacuum of endless abuse.

I don't allow liars in my life. I have no use for strong, silent types. They don't bring me joy. Communication is vital in relationships. If someone remains silent, they become a burden to the relationship. Passive-aggressive people often use the silent treatment as punishment when you don't comply with their control tactics. Their silence is a manipulation tactic intended to get you to do what they want. Some make backhanded, judgmental, snide, and sarcastic comments about others to shame you for the same behavior. They don't discuss the facts or resolve issues calmly. Instead, they resort to avoidance tactics, such as storming out of the house. They exude aggressiveness while appearing passive.

Aggressive people display rude and cruel behavior. Many are abusive with their words, vulgarity, and even in their manner of walking. They call you hurtful names to your face. They are bullies on the road and drive with road rage. Watching someone drive can reveal a lot about who they are. To them, this is their earth. How dare you set foot on their soil? This is their house. You are lucky to have a place to sleep. They keep you in fear by threatening physical violence. Many of them carry out those threats.

Our gut is our inner child. Always listen to your gut. You can change your mind later if your gut tells you something different. If it feels wrong, then it's wrong. If it feels bad, then it's bad. If it feels hurtful, then it's hurtful.

If someone is acting aloof or rude, it's probably true. However, it might have nothing to do with you. It's best to check before reacting. If they remain aloof when you see them again, you can bring up their behavior. Ask if there's anything they'd like to talk about. They might not be honest. However, we can let them know that if we've offended them, we're sorry. The more we learn to trust our gut, the better we can read people.

We can compare abusive people to a broken toaster. Whenever you buy a toaster, always keep your receipt. Return the broken ones to the store immediately for a refund. Tell them you're returning it because it only produces burnt toast! Learn to recognize harmful behavior quickly. Then we won't waste our time buying a broken toaster in the first place.

It's important to please our Heavenly Father. To make our Poppa happy, we must love Him, ourselves, and others. He is also the *wind beneath my wings.* Me and God, two peas in a pod.

Having a relationship with Father has brought me much peace. I talk to Him, trust Him, and look forward to being with Him forever. Being a leader for love is important to me. When my flesh falls away, who am I? We all have a choice of heaven or hell. I've taken charge of my journey. I'm climbing the staircase to heaven. Putting on my *wings,* I'm flying high and *sailing* onto the high seas.

I feel strong knowing that Poppa has my back. We all deserve His love. A perfect Father shows perfect love to all His children. He knows we all make mistakes. He's patient and understanding as we stumble through this weed-filled world. I'm comforted knowing He's waiting for me on the other side of life's waterfall.

Throughout the years, I have focused on my spirituality. My ultimate goal is to enter the *Pearly Gates* of heaven. Although I've thoroughly studied the Bible, I don't consider myself a religious person. Instead, I see myself as spiritual only. We're all spiritual beings on a spiritual journey. I'm not a member of any church. I'm only a member of the many-membered body of Jesus. We don't need a building for that. The only name I go by is Christian — or Christ-woman.

I've learned that grace grants us entry into heaven. I've also come to understand that grace has no connection to the blessings or rewards we will receive. Poppa promised us rewards, which are payments for the good works we do for Him. I don't know exactly what His blessings and rewards are, but He said we will receive fine linen garments. The more righteous acts we perform now, the greater the rewards we will receive.

I'm not a materialistic person. However, I look forward to receiving His wheelbarrows full of wonderful blessings. I will be like a kid in a candy store. If I know Him, and if He knows me, He'll have a cute little pink flying saucer waiting for me. Besides that, He will give me some fun jobs to do. My goal is for him to be proud of me. I never want to be one of the basic kids. I want to shine for Him like a bright and shining star. He and I will share hugs and exchange lots of high-fives when I get to heaven.

Being His servant means loving Him, ourselves, and others. We all desire genuine love. He doesn't want fake love either. Authentic love is the answer — every time. He smiles when I love His other children. Who wouldn't want to love and please our Poppa? He owns everything in the universe.

Many people try to flatter a wealthy person here on earth, hoping they'll share their riches. But they forget to butter up our Heavenly Poppa. He's the one who literally owns everything. That includes all the temporary possessions that rich people have. Loving our Poppa, ourselves, and others truly pleases Him. Choosing His path of love is the only way to enter His *Pearly Gates.*

I've learned how to use my weed whacker. However, I know Poppa's weed whacker works the best. He'll whack the roots so the harmful weeds never grow back. He doesn't want to whack them. That's why He has servants to encourage them to choose love. Since Poppa doesn't wish to whack them, I have a lot of patience with them. I hope I can help them come around to Poppa's way of thinking — Poppa's path of love.

This world is simply a testing and proving ground so that Poppa can remove the harmful weeds. Knowing this gives me great patience. You can bet yer boots I'm looking forward to a happily ever after without weeds. We will either cut the mustard, or we cannot enter the *Pearly Gates* of heaven.

I look forward to enjoying eternal peace, joy, love, and happiness. It fills me with great excitement. It also gives me an unwavering resolve to continue putting one foot in front of the other until I reach my destination. I already feel as if I live in peace, joy, love, and happiness because I know my happily ever after is just around the corner. Often, I feel like a kid counting down the days to the biggest and best Christmas morning ever — that's the morning I'll get to be with my Poppa.

Having a relationship with Poppa is the most valuable *hidden treasure* to seek. It gives me great purpose and immense joy to serve Him. Knowing I have an important purpose excites me to get out of bed each morning. I have work to do for my Poppa! I let Him *sail my ship* when He has something for me to do.

Many days when I wake up, I ask Him, "Poppa, what can I do for you today? How can I help your other children?" Being on a path of loving and pleasing our Poppa brings me great peace and happiness. I'm only a 10 on my happiness scale because I have this wonderful and beautiful relationship with Him. Without Him, I'd only be a five. He's my best friend. I'm my best friend. Livvy is my best friend. That makes us three peas in a pod.

~ Cutting Through the Fog ~

Birds of a feather flock together. What type of birds are we flying with? What does that say about us? Loving ourselves doesn't mean being friends with negative, vulgar, or cruel people. They corrupt and harm us. Those who are cruelest to others love themselves the least. It's important to *cut through the fog.* We need to recognize who is good for us and who isn't.

Gossipers hurt others with negative, judgmental, and critical behavior. I don't trust them, so I keep my distance. They are two-faced and have split personalities. If they gossip to us about others, you can bet yer boots they'll gossip about us to others. We're not special to them. Many gossipers pretend to like us just to gather information. As soon as they leave, they'll gossip behind our backs.

I stay consistent in my stance against gossip. Gossipers aren't my friends. They are passing around goose juice. We won't lose a friend by speaking out against gossip. I also stand up for the person the gossiper is attacking. The bonus is that they'll let others know how I feel about gossiping. They can't help themselves.

Sarcasm is a form of passive-aggressive behavior. This cruel person will claim they were only joking. Did anyone laugh? Using sarcasm to belittle others is rude behavior. It shows a better-than-thou attitude toward others. These people have a haughty, vain, conceited, and prideful love for themselves. They are on an ego trip and believe themselves superior to everyone. They use sarcasm to hide their underlying anger and contempt for others. I never laugh at their cruel and rude behavior. Laughing would make me part of their cruelty. If they had respect and love for themselves, they would love and respect others.

Everyone chooses who they are. The path of love is easy. Pick a side. We stand either for good and love or for bad and hate. We cannot find peace by having one foot in both worlds. Love spreads peace, joy, compassion, caring, patience, and understanding. Hate includes rude, cruel, offensive, crude, vulgar, sarcastic, filthy-minded, perverted, judgmental, critical, gossiping, backbiting, and condescending behavior.

We'll all make it through this life — one way or another. It becomes easier if we remove all harmful things and people from our lives. What enters our eyes and ears comes out of our mouths. If what goes in is corrupt, then corruption comes out. If good things go in, then good things come out.

To *cut through the fog* and eliminate harmful things and people from our lives, we must first identify them. Burnt toast includes, but isn't limited to: sarcasm, gossip, backbiting, judging, criticizing, condescending behavior, hierarchy, manipulation, hatred, rudeness, lying, cheating, stealing, yelling, arguing, bullying, road rage, rape, molestation, murder, vulgarity, cursing, gambling, perversion, pornography, vulgar or inappropriate music and shows, drugs, alcoholism, aggressive and passive-aggressive behavior, negativity, laziness, procrastination, disrespect, unreliability, irresponsibility, being unapologetic, and refusal to take responsibility for one's actions.

Adding delightful brown buttery toast to our lives includes, but is not limited to: loving ourselves, finding projects to do, fixing things, reading a book, getting enough sleep, painting by numbers, writing a book, learning to play the piano, becoming a home chef, taking care of our home, our car, and our children, playing games, being a better spouse, finding a hobby we enjoy, learning a new skill, growing a garden, or listening to soft, peaceful, and loving music.

We have forever and plenty of time to enjoy whatever we're doing. Whether we're washing the dishes or vacuuming the floor, doing laundry, or going to the store, we should praise ourselves after each task. Receiving praise motivates us to act more responsibly to earn more praise. We love feeling good about ourselves and our achievements. When you give yourself praise, it will amaze you how many things you can accomplish now. You'll crave more of this wonderful feeling that comes from praising yourself for a job well done.

People give in to peer pressure because they haven't learned how to say "no, thank you." They lack confidence and assertiveness. Many want to appear cool to their friends. They want to be accepted and loved by others. Many have fallen into the trap of pleasing others. Instead, they should do what is best for themselves. The more we focus on loving ourselves, the less we'll fall for peer pressure. Being our own best friend is all we need. Anyone pressuring us to do something against our gut instinct isn't a true friend.

In using love and praise toward ourselves, we build confidence in who we are. Those wanting us to do bad things are not friends. We don't need to fear standing up for what is right. Be a shining star. Be the light that this dark world needs.

When we choose self-love, it boosts our confidence. Then we realize that everything we say and do is based on love. That can never be wrong. We then see that loving ourselves and standing up for ourselves is the right thing to do.

Skilled defensive driving is crucial as we navigate the roads of life. Our journey will have many curves, hills, speed bumps, and potholes. We need to watch our blind spots and be prepared to swerve around aggressive drivers who might hit, hurt, or harm us emotionally. Many road bullies act out of road rage. Sometimes, they tail us closely, trying to intimidate or control us. Other times, they run us off the road. They make our heads spin as they speed past, leaving rubber marks on our hearts. It's safer to choose a different route to avoid these abusive drivers and stay safe.

There's always a bully, scammer, or thief nearby. If it sounds too good to be true, it probably is. If we leave a $20 bill out in the open, someone will steal it. Someone is always looking to take advantage of us. Our pain becomes their gain. People in general have become corrupt. Many are wearing masks and hiding their true selves. Television, music, and social media have corrupted, infiltrated, and propagandized many into doing harmful behavior. Many have become desensitized to hurting others. They are being programmed to exhibit this behavior.

I have achieved peace and tranquility by removing the sources of anxiety from my life. I don't participate in social media, and I rarely watch TV. I keep my space quiet and peaceful. I don't listen to vulgar music. I'm aware of the purpose of ads — they are propaganda. Owning a specific material item will not bring me happiness. It won't make me better than others. I find peace and joy within myself rather than from external sources.

The more we love ourselves, the less we will worry about what others think about us. I don't need frivolous items to survive. I take pride in being frugal and wise with my money. I don't worship or idolize people or material possessions. I'm not jealous when the neighbor gets a new car.

Our Heavenly Father doesn't want us to worship people, preachers, celebrities, or objects. He desires that we worship, admire, and love Him. True joy comes from focusing on what Poppa promotes rather than what the material world pushes at us. It doesn't matter what items we own. What matters is that we're pleasing to our Father in heaven.

~ Waves of Freedom ~

Loving ourselves includes striving to be as healthy as possible. Over the years, I've taken vitamins, eaten nutritious food, and maintained a healthy weight. I use a TENS unit or a back machine to relieve tension in my neck and back when needed. I've also performed colon and parasite cleanses.

Focusing on our emotional health is essential to discovering peace, joy, love, and happiness. Life is our unique personal adventure. Compared to forever, we're only on Earth for a short time. It's best to enjoy every moment. Make the best of it.

I've made many decisions and mistakes along the way. Some choices were good, while others made me want to crawl under a rug. I've learned something from every decision and mistake I've made. What I've learned is the silver lining. The silver lining is that I now know better. Plus, I can use what I've learned to help others. Always look for the silver lining.

Maintaining a healthy brain is essential. Think of it as a dinner table. Our table is the emotional center of our brain. It's full of dirty dishes, representing our fears, traumas, hurts, and abuses. I take each dirty dish to the sink. I wash it with tears. Next, I dry it with love and understanding. Then I put it away as a silver lining in my memory.

Holding onto life's traumas, hurts, and pains in our emotional center is harmful to our well-being. As it fills up, it affects how we react to future situations. We respond to upcoming issues and circumstances with heightened emotion. Our emotional center overrides our ability to think clearly. It's crucial to process, store, and release those hurts and pains into our memory center so that we can respond calmly to people in the future.

To clear our emotional center, it takes courage and love. We also need the willingness to cry. Tears are a miracle and one of the best healing therapies our Father has given us. It's His gift to help us release built-up emotions. There's great strength in tears. Every time we cry, we reach a deeper level of understanding and wisdom. I never hold back when I feel like crying. That would mean denying my inner child something she needs. That's not loving myself.

Some fathers have taught their boys to be macho. They say that a real man doesn't cry. They are mistaken and have lied to their sons. Jesus wept. Are they calling Jesus a wimp? Jesus is tender and gentle. He feels all His emotions and expresses them freely. He cries when His heart feels like crying. His left boot is courage. His right boot is love. He said we have to become like little children to enter the kingdom of heaven. That means we must let go of all pompous, haughty, and macho behavior. We must become humble, gentle, and able to cry.

If we don't clear our emotional center, we will continue to function in a constant state of fight-or-flight, reacting emotionally to situations rather than responding rationally. We will avoid confrontation and run away rather than assertively stand up for ourselves. We must examine each dish individually. It's essential to acknowledge the pain and cry if needed. Then, if possible, apologize to those we've hurt and to ourselves if necessary. Find the silver lining — what have we learned from it? Be thankful for the lesson, then store it in our long-term memory.

After finding the silver lining, be thankful for the lesson. It gives us the gift of deeper understanding and wisdom. We didn't walk away empty-handed. After experiencing many traumas, I now view adverse events as opportunities for growth and learning. It also gives me more practice in being assertive. Standing up for myself is now fun. I no longer try to escape negative experiences. I'll get some excellent target practice and learn something from every experience. In the end, I added another silver coin of wisdom to my pocket.

I turn negative experiences into gratitude for the coin. I feel proud because I stood up for Livvy. Now she sees me as her hero. I've gained more confidence by standing my ground and not letting others cross my boundaries. I can now analyze how to improve next time.

Finding the silver lining gets easier with practice. Gratitude replaces heartache. Feeling grateful for lessons learned is a key to emotional freedom. After much practice, I no longer need to find the silver lining right away. I observe each situation and respond assertively. I know there's always a silver lining. It's like knowing there's dirt in the ground or gold at the end of every rainbow. The silver lining is the pot of gold. It's there every time. To find the silver lining, ask yourself how this hurt and pain could be a positive thing. What lesson has this experience taught you? How can you help others because of this experience?

I analyze every thought, feeling, and behavior. Why am I feeling this way? How did that experience make me feel? What is causing this anxiety? My thoughts and feelings are valuable tools for growth. They are the water my garden needs to flourish. I allow them freely to enter my mind. I'm never afraid of them. I don't push them away. They are simply thoughts and feelings. They can't hurt me. I ponder and reflect on everything. I come to a clear understanding of myself and exactly who I am. Once we see clearly who we are, we can eliminate what we don't want, and we can love the person we choose to become. As long as we strive to improve every day, we can love and respect the person we are working hard to be.

No matter what I'm feeling, I always talk to my Livvy. I say, *Livvy, I'm sorry you're feeling this way. *What's going on? *What exactly is causing this tightness or heaviness in your chest? *Livvy, why are you feeling so overwhelmed? *Liv, why are you feeling anxious? *Livvy, why are you feeling sad? I'm in tune with and trust myself. I'm aware of what's bothering me. Deep down, I know exactly how to make it better. With courage, I acknowledge it and bring it to the sink. I must wash that dish so mold and bacteria don't grow into my heart, mind, and soul.

I'm honest with myself. I'm a best friend to my inner child, and help her overcome her fears, sadness, stress, anxiety, and pain. Livvy will be honest with me if she trusts that I won't hurt her. Then, together, we explore different options to solve our problem. We throw some solutions against the wall to see what sticks. Then we pick the one that seems most effective. We try it, and if it works, great! If not, I go back to the drawing board with Livvy. We keep trying. I must wash that dish.

I've found several ways to wash, dry, and store my dishes in my memory center. One method is Womb Therapy, and the other involves gently tapping on my energy points.

Womb Therapy consists of a 10-minute quiet meditation. Closing my eyes, I imagine I'm Livvy's mom. I travel back in time to the moment I first learned I was pregnant with Livvy. I picture myself raising her, being her best friend, and giving her all the love, comfort, and praise she deserves. Then, I bring the meditation to the present day. Being creative, envision many wonderful moments for yourself. Give yourself lots of love. It goes something like this:

*Oh, wow! I'm pregnant with a girl! This is incredible! How exciting! Aww, I'm sure she'll be a precious little one — a bundle of joy. I hope I will be a great mom. I should name her Olivia. That sounds pretty. I'll call her Livvy for short. Oh, my belly is getting so big! Dear Lord, she kicked me! Livvy, hello sweetheart. I'm excited to see you. It won't be too much longer now, and you'll be here. I'd better get you some clothes and diapers.

Livvy, you're finally here! I've been waiting for you, baby cakes. Look at you! You're beautiful! Oh, just look at those adorable fingers and toes. I want to cuddle with you all the time. I'll take good care of you. You deserve the best mommy in the world. I love you so much. You're a sweet little princess. Here, let me rock you and sing songs to you.

I can't believe how much you've grown. You're about to start kindergarten already. I'm glad we made it through those messy years. But look at you now — walking, talking, and beautiful as ever! I am so proud of you! You're the best kid ever, Livvy! You're so smart and kind. Nobody could ask for a better child. Thank you, Livvy, for coming into my life.

Oh my goodness, time flies. You are becoming a teenager. I'm feeling upset about that boy being mean to you. I'll talk to your teacher to ensure she handles it correctly. You deserve kindness and respect. I'll make sure she punishes that naughty boy. You can talk to me about anything. I'll help you get through it. I'm your best friend. That's what friends are for. Nobody is going to hurt my sweet Livvy. You are doing great, Princess. I know it's tough. We'll get through this together.

You're getting married? I'm so happy for you. He's such a great guy. I know he'll take good care of you, too. We'll see each other often — after all, we're best friends. You will always be my little sweetie pie. I'm so proud of you. You are the most amazing person in the entire world. You are such a sweet and kind child. Thank you for loving me and sharing your life with me. I'll always take care of you. I'll never let anyone hurt you. You are my best friend, Livvy. I love you so much!*

Womb therapy meditation is healing. It helps us give ourselves the love, comfort, and praise we deserve — and should have received. It empowers us to recreate our experiences. We now receive the care we needed from the moment we entered our mother's womb. It also allows us to keep giving ourselves the love, comfort, and praise we still need today. Overall, it helps us take full responsibility for our own emotional self-care.

Another effective healing technique involves gentle tapping on our energy points. Using our first two fingers, we tap on each point. We examine all the dirty dishes on our table. Digging deep, we process them all. We also need to find the ones hiding under the table. All of those dirty dishes are causing a bzzzt in our energy system. We need to wash them all. They have mold and bacteria growing on them. Therefore, the soap and scrub brush they need are a gentle tapping. Meanwhile, we acknowledge the pain and give ourselves love and positive reinforcement.

Wash one emotional pain at a time. Tap until you feel a release happen. It usually takes only a minute or two. Then move on to the next dirty dish. You'll know the release has happened when you begin to feel bored. Sometimes, a new thought will pop into your mind.

The energy points I tap are the five on my face. 1) Inside corner of my eyebrow. 2) Outside corner of my eyebrow. 3) Just below my eye. 4) Directly beneath my nose. 5) Just below my lower lip. You can use either side of your face. Using two fingers, gently tap the inner eyebrow and work your way to the bottom lip. Tap 15-20 times on each point.

While tapping, acknowledge your pain, hurt, or trauma. Then finish the sentence with deep love for yourself. Keep tapping the entire time, even if you cry. Choose whichever dirty dish that enters your mind first. When you reach the lowest energy point, move back up to the top of the inner eyebrow again. Top to bottom, top to bottom, over and over. While tapping, put your dirty dish in the sink. Repeat your chosen statement until you feel the release happen.

Say something like this: "Even though my dad was abusive, I deeply and completely love myself." Repeatedly, say it silently or out loud. Continue tapping from top to bottom. It may take five times, or it might take twenty. It all depends on the severity of the trauma, or how stuck the gunk is on the dish that didn't get washed right away.

Once you feel the release, a new thought will come into your mind. Move on to the next dirty dish. You might say, "Even though I saw my dad attack my sister, Ella, I deeply and completely love myself." Say it repeatedly. Tap, tap, tap. When you feel the release, move on to the next dirty dish. You can tap on anything and everything. It's an effective healing tool for trauma, fear, worry, and emotional pain. It also helps with PTSD, phobias, and the death of a loved one. Here are some other examples:

Even though I feel sad, I deeply and completely love myself. *Even though that person hurt me, *Even though I feel scared, *Even though I feel overwhelmed, *Even though I feel anxious, *Even though I made this horrible mistake, *Even though I have this fear of spiders, *Even though so-and-so did such-and-such, *Even though I messed up on that one, I forgive myself, and I deeply and completely love myself.

Let your tears flow as you wash your dirty dishes. Allow yourself to cry as much as you need. Find the silver lining in what you've learned from this dish. Be thankful for the silver coin you can now add to your pocket. Dry your dishes with your towel of love for yourself. Release the dish and store it away in the cupboard, into the memory center of your brain. You don't want to forget what happened to you. That memory will help prevent it from happening again. The memory and the lesson learned will also give you the ability to help others in the future.

Remove all the bzzzts in your energy system. Then reach a deep understanding that no matter what anyone else has done or said to you — the only thing that matters is that "I deeply and completely love myself." That was them who did that. That is who they are. That is not me! I love me! I deserve love and kindness. No matter what they did, it's my job — and my job only — to deeply and completely love myself.

We've processed the bzzzts. Now, we can face each new situation with a clear mind. We can approach each new incident without our built-up emotions getting in the way. Trust me, there will be many more hurtful people who come into your life. It will hurt again. At least now you have a tool to help you process the bzzzts that people zap you with. Stay strong, be assertive, and stand up for yourself. Love yourself deeply and completely. Loving ourselves is our responsibility to our inner child. Buck up and take the bull by the horns. No fear. Protect and love little Livvy to the ends of the earth. She needs you.

You can also use tapping to instill positive beliefs into your heart, mind, and soul. It's a quick, positive brainwashing technique. While tapping, you can say, *Livvy, I love you. You are the best! *Livvy, I'm proud of you. You're doing a great job! *Livvy, I promise I'm going to protect you and never let anyone hurt you ever again! *Livvy, you are beautiful, intelligent, special, and important. You deserve the best.

Remove the noose that is choking you. Set yourself free. Sail out on the *waves of freedom.* Avoid hurtful or rude people. You don't need them — they only lower your happiness. If someone is hurting you, refuses to offer genuine apologies, won't take responsibility, argues, shifts blame onto you, or says you're overreacting — treat it as a mere business transaction. *Remove all emotionalism. *State the facts. *Share how you feel. *Clarify that you need an apology to continue the relationship. *If they don't give a sincere apology — patiently, calmly, confidently, assertively, respectfully, and lovingly — press your delete button.

True friends aren't hurtful. They respect your privacy and boundaries. They let you share what you want, and when you want. Genuine friends apologize if they hurt you. A real friend doesn't bat an eye if you choose to wear white or florals in the middle of winter.

To find peace, joy, love, and happiness, we need to remove all the dirty birds from our lives and wash our dirty dishes. It's best to keep our flower garden small to prevent it from becoming overrun with weeds. Loving ourselves wins every time.

I am Sunny Side Up — happy and free. I have filled my cup with love, and that love overflows to others. Genuine love can only spill over to others if we first love ourselves. I'll see you on the other side of the waterfall — when you too become Sunny Side Up.

Dear Livvy, despite overwhelming odds, you did an amazing job! I'm super proud of you. Great job, Livvy. I love you!

www.ingramcontent.com/pod-product-compliance
Lightning Source LLC
LaVergne TN
LVHW010945110826
845149LV00013B/2753

* 9 7 9 8 9 9 4 6 2 0 0 9 0 *